Create the Perfect Love Room on Airbnb

From Idea to Reality

By

Théo Labranche

Table of contents :

INTRODUCTION

You may have heard about those dreamy spaces popping up on Airbnb, those ideal romantic retreats, those Love Rooms that capture the imagination of travelers in search of special moments. You are about to delve into the fascinating world of creating a Love Room, a unique and ever-evolving opportunity for Airbnb hosts.

The Love Room is not just a place to stay; it's an experience, a romantic getaway designed to evoke emotions and create lasting memories. It caters to a growing need among travelers for magic, intimacy, and exceptional moments. If you're considering venturing into hospitality, whether you have an available property or are ready to invest in a dedicated space, this booklet is for you.

Throughout the pages, we will explore each step of the process, from the initial idea to creating a Love Room that not only wows your guests but also maximizes your income. You'll learn how to choose the ideal location, design enchanting decor, market your Love Room effectively, manage bookings, and much more.

Creating a Love Room on Airbnb is not just an opportunity to make money; it's a chance to turn your passion for hospitality into an authentic and memorable experience for your guests. Whether you're a novice or an experienced host, this guide will help you create the perfect Love Room and embark on this exciting adventure.

Get ready to dive into the world of love, dreams, and success on Airbnb. Welcome to the journey that will lead you to the creation of the ideal Love Room, an exceptional experience for couples in search of love and adventure.

Chapter 1: Understanding the Love Room

Definition and Characteristics of a Love Room

Discover the Love Room:

Let's start by understanding what a Love Room is. A Love Room is an accommodation space designed to create a romantic and intimate atmosphere. It stands out through its ambiance, decor, and amenities specifically crafted for couples in search of unforgettable moments. A Love Room can be a room in your own home or a standalone unit, but it must offer a unique romantic experience.

Enchanting Ambiance:

The key to a Love Room lies in its ambiance. It should evoke passion, love, and romance. This means soothing colors, soft lighting, high-quality linens, rose petals on the bed, scented candles, and perhaps a hot tub or jacuzzi.

Special Amenities:

Love Rooms also distinguish themselves through special amenities. Think of features such as a large ceiling mirror, a comfortable king-size bed, romantic background music, and perhaps accessories to spice up the night. These features contribute to the overall Love Room experience.

The Allure of Love Rooms for Travelers

A Romantic Getaway:

Travelers are increasingly seeking unique experiences, getaways that stand out. Love Rooms offer a perfect romantic escape for couples in search of special moments. They are a response to the monotony of traditional hotels.

Privacy and Discretion:

Love Rooms ensure a high level of privacy. Travelers appreciate the discretion of these spaces, where they can focus on their relationship without fear of disturbance. It's a haven for couples wanting to reconnect.

Unforgettable Experiences:

Love Rooms aim to create unforgettable memories. Travelers are looking to live romantic moments, and these spaces are designed to offer a memorable experience, be it for an anniversary, honeymoon, or just a special night.

Benefits of Offering a Love Room on Airbnb

Potential Income:

Love Rooms can generate substantial income. Couples are willing to pay more for a romantic and unique experience. By offering a Love Room, you have the opportunity to maximize your earnings.

Market Differentiation:

As an Airbnb host, offering a Love Room sets you apart from the competition. You attract a specific audience seeking a romantic experience. This can help you maintain a high occupancy rate. Guest Satisfaction: Offering a well-designed Love Room can result in positive reviews and build guest loyalty. Satisfied guests are more likely to return and recommend your space to other couples.

By understanding the characteristics, allure, and benefits of Love Rooms, you are ready to explore how to create the perfect Love Room on Airbnb. This chapter has provided you with a solid foundation for the rest of this guide, where we will delve into each aspect of this exciting process in detail.

Chapter 2: Finding the Ideal Location

Choosing the Location for Your Love Room

Strategic Thinking:

The crucial first step in creating a Love Room is choosing the ideal location. Consider where you want to establish your Love Room. Is it in a bustling city, a quaint small town, in the countryside, or near the beach? Identify the type of destination that aligns with the experience you want to offer.

Proximity to Attractions:

Consider the proximity to local attractions. Love Rooms located near romantic restaurants, tourist sites, or parks offer a more comprehensive experience to travelers. Think about what your location can offer your guests in terms of entertainment and amenities.

Competition:

Examine the competition in the area. Healthy competition can indicate demand for this type of accommodation. However, make sure to offer something unique to stand out from other hosts.

Legal and Regulatory Considerations for Love Room Rentals

When embarking on Love Room rentals, it's crucial to be well-versed in legal and regulatory aspects across different regions. Here are key considerations applicable universally:

Compliance with Local Laws:

Understand and comply with local regulations governing short-term rentals. This includes obtaining necessary permits, adhering to zoning laws, and meeting specific requirements set by local authorities.

Tax Implications:

Stay informed about the tax implications associated with renting out your Love Room. Ensure compliance with tax obligations related to this activity, including income declaration and any applicable tourist taxes.

Safety and Construction Standards:

Prioritize the safety of your guests by ensuring that your Love Room meets current safety and construction standards. This encompasses features like fire safety measures, emergency exits, and adherence to electrical installation standards.

Being attentive to these legal and regulatory considerations sets the foundation for a successful and compliant Love Room rental experience, regardless of the country or region.

The Importance of Location in Attracting Travelers

Influence on Travelers' Decisions:

Location is one of the primary factors influencing travelers' decisions. An ideal location can be the starting point for an unforgettable experience. Make sure to highlight the strengths of your location in your listing, whether it's panoramic views, proximity to the beach, or easy access to local attractions.

Customize Your Listing:

Showcase the advantages of your location in your Airbnb listing. Highlight what makes your neighborhood special, nearby activities, romantic restaurants, and unique places your guests can explore.

<u>**Accurate Images and Descriptions:**</u>

Use accurate images and descriptions to present your location. Show photos of the neighborhood, panoramic views, and indicate the distance to local attractions. Travelers appreciate transparency and authenticity.

By carefully choosing the location of your Love Room and adhering to local regulations, you lay the groundwork for a successful experience for your guests. The rest of this guide will help you go further in creating your Love Room on Airbnb.

Chapter 3: Designing and Decorating the Love Room

Creating a Romantic and Intimate Ambiance

The Essence of a Love Room:

The key to any Love Room is to create a romantic and intimate ambiance. Use soothing colors and warm tones to evoke passion. Opt for soft lighting with adjustable lamps to set the mood. Scented candles can add a magical touch to the overall atmosphere.

The Power of Details:

Details make the difference. Don't forget rose petals on the bed, plush cushions, high-quality linens, and blackout curtains to create an intimate environment. Ensure that every element in the room contributes to the romantic ambiance you want to create.

Decoration and Layout Tips

Romantic Theme:

Choose a romantic decor theme that aligns with the ambiance you want to create. It could be a rustic, nautical, urban, or any theme that evokes romance. Ensure that all decor elements, from paintings to rugs, harmonize with this theme.

Elegant Furniture:

Opt for stylish and comfortable furniture. A king-size bed with a padded headboard is a must for a Love Room. The furniture should be of high quality and offer superior comfort for guests.

<u>**Strategic Mirrors:**</u>

A strategically placed mirror on the ceiling or wall can add a sensual dimension to the room. It creates a unique visual effect and can be a surprising element for travelers.

Selection of Appropriate Furniture and Accessories

<u>**Jacuzzi or Hot Tub:**</u>

If space allows, a jacuzzi or hot tub can be an exceptional addition to a Love Room. Ensure it is well-maintained and always ready for use.

<u>**Ambient Music:**</u>

Provide guests with the opportunity to create the perfect sound ambiance. Make available a quality audio system with a selection of romantic ambient music.

<u>**Sensual Extras:**</u>

If desired, offer sensual extras such as massage oils, additional rose petals, or accessories to spice up the evening. Ensure these items are of high quality and well-maintained.

By creating a romantic atmosphere and choosing the right furniture and accessories, you can design a Love Room that meets your guests' expectations for intimacy and romance. This chapter has provided essential tips to transform your space into an unforgettable experience for couples seeking romance.

Chapter 4: Marketing and Promotion

Creating an Appealing Airbnb Listing

Irresistible Title:

The title of your listing is the first thing travelers see. Use catchy words to describe your Love Room, such as "Romantic Retreat" or "Magical Night for Two."

Detailed Descriptions:

Write a detailed description of your Love Room, highlighting its ambiance, special features, and what makes it unique. Also, describe the amenities you offer, such as the jacuzzi or rose petals.

<u>**Quick Responses:**</u>

Be responsive to messages and booking requests. Travelers appreciate prompt responses and the host's availability.

Using High-Quality Photos to Showcase Your Love Room

<u>**Professional Photography:**</u>

Hire a professional photographer or use quality equipment to take photos of your Love Room. Well-lit and attractive images are essential for attracting travelers.

<u>**Capture the Ambiance:**</u>

Your photos should capture the romantic ambiance of the room. Use soft lighting to create a warm atmosphere, and ensure that beds and special amenities are highlighted.

<u>**Detail Photos:**</u>

Don't forget to photograph important details, such as the bed with rose petals, the hot tub, and sensual accessories. These images can generate excitement among travelers.

Pricing Strategies to Maximize Revenue

Dynamic Pricing:

Use dynamic pricing to automatically adjust prices based on demand and seasonal periods. You can charge more for popular nights, weekends, and holidays.

Special Packages:

Offer special packages for special occasions, such as Valentine's Day or anniversaries. These packages may include extras like roses, chocolates, or massages.

Last-Minute Deals:

If you have short-term unbooked dates, offer last-minute discounts to attract spontaneous travelers.

Rewards for Loyal Guests:

Encourage guest loyalty by offering discounts or benefits for travelers who return to stay in your Love Room.

By creating an irresistible listing, using high-quality photos, and implementing a smart pricing strategy, you increase your chances of attracting travelers to your Love Room. Effective promotion of your space is essential to boost your occupancy rate and revenue.

Chapter 5: Management and Customer Service

Guest Reception and Reservation Management

Effective Communication:

Respond promptly to inquiries and reservations. Communication is essential to reassure travelers and address their questions.

Warm Welcome:

Ensure the smooth arrival of travelers. Be punctual, welcoming, and ready to guide them to your Love Room. Explain special amenities and be prepared to meet their needs.

Useful Information:

Provide travelers with useful information, such as a local guide to romantic restaurants, couple activities, and tips to make the most of their stay.

Cleaning and Maintenance of the Love Room

High Cleanliness Standards:

Maintain high cleanliness standards in your Love Room. Ensure everything is spotless upon travelers' arrival. Cleaning should include changing sheets, washing towels, and deep cleaning the bathroom.

Regular Maintenance:

Ensure all amenities, including the jacuzzi, are in good working condition. Promptly repair anything damaged or defective.

Quality Control:

Conduct regular quality checks to ensure everything is in order. This may include weekly checks to ensure lighting is functioning correctly and sensual accessories are well-stocked.

Offering Special Services and Experiences for Guests

Romantic Extras:

Offer romantic extras such as massages, romantic bubble baths, or candlelit dinners that travelers can book in addition to their stay.

Personalized Concierge:

Provide personalized concierge assistance by helping travelers organize special activities, such as a sunset cruise or a wine tasting in the area.

Feedback and Follow-Up:

After travelers depart, seek feedback on their stay and consider their suggestions.

Use this feedback to continuously improve the experience you offer.

By offering a warm welcome, maintaining the cleanliness and condition of your Love Room, and providing special services and experiences, you create an exceptional experience for your guests. Customer satisfaction is essential to retain travelers and strengthen your reputation as a quality Love Room host.

Chapter 6: Maximizing Revenue and Evolving

How to Analyze the Performance of Your Love Room

Review of Feedback:

Carefully monitor traveler feedback to identify strengths and areas for improvement. Use this information for ongoing improvements.

Key Performance Indicators (KPIs):

Identify KPIs such as occupancy rate, average nightly price, and monthly revenue. Track this data to assess the performance of your Love Room.

<u>**Surveys and Questionnaires:**</u>

Solicit traveler feedback through surveys or questionnaires to gain valuable insights into their experience. Use these responses to adjust your offerings.

Strategies to Increase Revenue Over Time

<u>**Pricing Review:**</u>

Regularly review your rates based on seasonal demand, local events, and market trends. Experiment with special rates for romantic packages and last-minute deals.

<u>**Customer Loyalty:**</u>

Encourage customer loyalty by offering discounts or benefits to returning travelers. Loyal customers are more likely to book again and recommend your Love Room.

<u>**Local Collaborations:**</u>

Establish partnerships with local businesses, such as restaurants, spas, or bike rental services, to offer special packages to travelers. This can enhance the value of your offering.

Considerations for Expansion or Diversification

Demand Evaluation:

If you are considering adding more Love Rooms to your offering, assess demand in your area. Ensure that the market can support expansion.

Offer Diversification:

Consider diversifying your offerings by providing different types of romantic rooms or accommodations, such as cottages, panoramic view suites, or romantic beach stays.

Quality Maintenance:

Regardless of your decision to expand or diversify, ensure you maintain the quality and consistency of the romantic experience you offer. Quality is crucial for customer loyalty.

By regularly analyzing the performance of your Love Room, implementing strategies to increase revenue, and considering options for expansion or diversification, you can maximize your earnings over time. Stay flexible and responsive to the changing needs of your customers and the market to continue thriving in the Love Room sector on Airbnb.

CONCLUSION

Congratulations, you have embarked on an exciting journey through the world of Love Rooms on Airbnb. You have discovered how to create an exceptional romantic experience for couples seeking unforgettable moments. So, what can you take away from this guide?

Love Rooms are more than just accommodation; they are romantic retreats designed to evoke emotions and create lasting memories.

Location is crucial. Choose the location for your Love Room carefully and ensure compliance with local regulations.

The design and decoration of your space are essential to create the romantic atmosphere sought by travelers.

Promoting your Love Room requires an attractive listing, high-quality photos, and strategic pricing.

Management and customer service play a key role in traveler satisfaction. Ensure you provide a memorable experience for every guest.

To maximize revenue over time, monitor performance, adjust pricing, encourage customer loyalty, and consider options for expansion or diversification.

When venturing into the world of Love Rooms on Airbnb, remember that every detail matters. Create a space that evokes emotions, inspires dreams, and allows couples to experience magical moments. Your passion for romantic hospitality can become a rewarding source of income.

So, get ready to welcome love-struck couples and offer them a romantic experience they will cherish forever. May your Love Room become the place where love dreams come true, and each visit is a new love story. Good luck in your journey of creating Love Rooms, and may each stay be an unforgettable romantic escape!